Original title:
Serenity by the Sea

Copyright © 2025 Creative Arts Management OÜ
All rights reserved.

Author: Cameron Blair
ISBN HARDBACK: 978-1-80581-524-2
ISBN PAPERBACK: 978-1-80581-051-3
ISBN EBOOK: 978-1-80581-524-2

Ripples of Peace at Waterside

A seagull stole my sandwich quick,
I laughed and thought, what a slick trick.
The waves are dancing, oh so spry,
While I just watch, a seagull's high.

Beachcombers hunt for shells galore,
But trip on flip-flops, hit the floor.
The tide comes in with a gentle sway,
As kids yell 'shark!'—gotta run away.

Echoes of Solitude in the Surf

I sat alone with ice-cream cone,
But seagulls believed I should be throne.
They landed near, with eyes so wide,
In hopes my treat they could abide.

The whispers of the waves so mild,
Reminds me of my inner child.
Yet every splash disturbs my nap,
Who knew the sea could be a trap?

A Canvas Painted in Blue Hues

Horizon stretches, shades of cheer,
But my umbrella just won't stay here.
It flips and flops, like a fish on land,
While I try to hunt some grains of sand.

The sun just smiles, a mischievous glee,
As I wrestle to keep my hat, you see.
The beach ball bounces, hits me hard,
I laugh along, like it's my yard.

Daysdreams Adrift on Driftwood

On driftwood boats, we sail away,
But ah! The tide thought it was play.
My friends all giggle, splashes fly,
As we embark on dreams nearby.

The skies are blue, but somehow gray,
When sunscreen sprays get tossed my way.
I'd call for help, but you see, it's fun,
To watch chaos under the sun.

Daydreams on the Water's Surface

Waves giggle as they roll,
Splashing thoughts of a laughing shoal.
A fish with a hat swims on by,
Making sure no one is dry.

Seagulls chat with a sassy flair,
Discussing the latest beachwear.
Sunbathers dance with sunblock on,
While crabs critique their moves at dawn.

The Solace Found in Gentle Swells

Bobbing like a cork in flight,
A jellyfish wearing shades, what a sight!
Seashells gossip near the shore,
While starfish plot to start a tour.

Waves hum a melody so sweet,
As turtles shuffle their little feet.
Starfish sing, 'We're just taking a break,
Please don't poke us; we're not a cake!'

Embracing the Quiet Currents

A clam takes selfies with a filter,
While a dolphin swims with a sassy tilt.
The calm waters hold secret laughs,
As octopuses draft jellyfish crafts.

In the shade of a wise old tree,
Crabs hold court with a cup of tea.
While they discuss the tide's next rise,
A clam yells, 'I found a pearly prize!'

Gulls in Flight, Free Spirits

Gulls soar high with a snack attack,
Bolting after treats, they don't hold back.
With wings spread wide and beaks agape,
They're plotting the best beach escape.

One gull says, 'Let's make a mess!'
Of picnic blankets, what a success!
As beachgoers laugh and chase them around,
'Next time, we'll guard our food; let's be profound!'

Moonlit Walks on Whispering Sands

The moon peeks down with a cheeky grin,
Crabs dance around like they're all-in.
Flip-flops left behind in a race,
Tripping over seaweed—what a disgrace!

Tides rolling in with a splash and a roar,
Seagulls stealing fries—what a score!
Laughter echoes as the waves play tag,
We chase our hats when the breezes wag!

Calm Reflections in Deep Aqua

Mirror-like waters, so still and bright,
Fish swim by wearing sunglasses, quite a sight!
A dolphin waves, "Hey, come join my spree!"
We try to dive, but just float like a bee!

Seashells giggle, tales whisper in waves,
Conch shells bragging about their brave saves.
A crab holds court, wearing a tiny crown,
"Listen up, folks! I'm royalty now!"

Daydreams upon the Sea Breeze

Kites flying high, tangled in laughter,
While dogs chase tails, they think it's a disaster.
Sandcastles crumbling with a soft little sigh,
"Who built this thing?" the seagulls cry!

The sun winks down, setting the scene,
We sipped iced tea, feeling quite keen.
But then—oh no! A wave gives a lurch,
And our picnic blanket takes quite a perch!

Finding Home in Ocean's Arms

A cozy cabana, so bright and cheery,
But in came the wind, making us leery.
Sunscreen battles, who's burning bright red?
Our hats take flight—oh, where are they headed?

A treasure hunt led by the gulls' loud cheer,
Finding lost flip-flops—oh dear, oh dear!
In the calm of waves, with laughter as bait,
We claim this place—it's our silly estate!

A Dance of Light on the Water's Surface

Sunbeams skip like kids on sand,
Waves crash, but they've no plan.
Seagulls squawk with jokes in tow,
Who knew the tide could steal the show?

Bubbles pop like party hats,
Fish flash smiles, wearing cool spats.
Crabs dance sideways, that's their charm,
While jellyfish float, raising alarm.

An old man tries to cast his line,
His hat's too big, it looks so fine.
But fish are laughing, swimming free,
They've planned a great escape, you see?

Shells whisper secrets, oh so bright,
As shadows stretch into the night.
The moon chuckles, winks at me,
What a riot, this salty spree!

Beachcomber's Serenity

Wandering feet find treasures rare,
A flip-flop's lost, but who can care?
A beach ball bounces, eager to play,
Dreams drift like clouds on a sunny day.

Seashells giggle, tucked in my bag,
I trip on seaweed, oh what a drag!
A crab makes faces, none too shy,
Laughing at me as I stumble by.

In the shade of a friendly palm,
I sip from a drink, all sweet and calm.
But a rogue wave creeps, a sneaky tease,
Soaked to the bone, oh what a breeze!

With sandy toes, I raise a cheer,
Living the dream, nothing to fear.
The ocean tickles, a bubbly tease,
Life's a beach, let's do this with ease!

Embracing the Vast and Endless Blue

Waves tumble in, a frothy delight,
Where mermaids laugh, out of sight.
A dolphin grins, takes a bow,
Saying, 'Come join the fun somehow!'

Kites soar high, like birds on leave,
While I chase dreams, tucked up my sleeve.
A sunburned nose, oh what a sight,
This beach bum's charm, oh so bright!

Towels spread like colorful dreams,
Laughter echoes, bursts at the seams.
I build a castle, oh what a feat,
Only to find it's a seat for my feet.

As sunset spills its colors wide,
I chuckle with joy, nothing to hide.
The vastness calls, wild and true,
In this wonderland, I just might fly too!

Harboring Peace Within

A boat with no anchor, it dances away,
Seagulls take selfies, they brighten the day.
Laughter floats gently on the brisk salty air,
Fish tell the best jokes, if you stop and just stare.

Flip-flops are tripping on the warm sandy ground,
Waves wink with chuckles, and giggles abound.
The tide brings a message, it's funny and light,
Even crabs share punchlines in the soft twilight.

Nature's Subtle Whisper

The breeze has a secret, it tickles my cheek,
Whispers of fun, in a language unique.
Palm trees are swaying, they're shaking a leg,
And sunbathers giggle like a tickled old beg.

A crab in a tux, marching proud as can be,
He sips on a cocktail while curled by a tree.
The ocean's a jester, a playful charade,
With waves making faces, in water parade.

Mornings Wrapped in Ocean's Embrace

Morning's first light brings a dance on the shore,
I watch the waves wobble, can't help but adore.
Squawking old pelicans gossip like pros,
With coffee in hand, the day joyously grows.

The surf's a comedian with jokes from afar,
Tickling toes, saying, 'Oh, look, I'm a star!'
Seashells are giggling beneath the sun's rays,
While dolphins juggle tales in their splashy displays.

Chasing Shadows Beneath the Waves

Shadows are playing beneath the bright sun,
They twist and they tangle, oh, what goofy fun!
The sandcastles laugh as the tide creeps on in,
While eels in tuxedos dance with a grin.

Clams hold their breath, when the whale starts to sing,
It's a concert of frolic, oh, what joy it brings!
Bubbles pop like laughter, as fish swim around,
In this watery wonder, pure joy can be found.

Sands of Time and Tranquility

Footprints fade as tides do play,
Crabs will dance in their own way.
Seagulls squawk like clowns in flight,
Waves tickle toes, oh what a sight!

Picnics turn to lunch for flies,
Sandcastles fall, much to our sighs.
But in laughter, joy is found,
As we trip and roll on sandy ground.

Solitude Wrapped in Ocean Waves

Alone I sit, but wait, who's that?
A fish that mocks my sun hat!
Waves come crashing, making a fuss,
While I sip tea, sharing with a bus!

The wind whispers jokes, oh so sly,
As crabs parade, strutting by.
With each splash, the ocean speaks,
Even my drink takes a salty leak!

The Beauty of Wandering Comets

Stars fall down like beach ball dreams,
Splashing light in cosmic beams.
Fish yell, "Hey, look at that glow!"
As jellyfish twirl in their flow.

On the shore we gaze with glee,
'Did you see that? Was it a spree?'
With giggles shared like skyward raves,
We'll recount tales from other waves.

Glistening Secrets in Shallow Depths

Treasures lie where the sunlight gleams,
But shells just giggle, or so it seems.
"Dive down deep!" the octopus grins,
While I ponder where my swimsuit begins!

But underfoot, there's dancing sand,
With starfish practicing their band.
"You call this shallow?" I jest with fright,
As a wave slaps back, my day's highlight!

Finding Zen in the Azure Deep

I sat on a wave, quite a move,
As seagulls danced and started to groove.
My towel flew off with a laugh and a kick,
While sand stuck in places, oh boy, what a trick!

Splashing around with a big, silly grin,
I searched for my zen, but where to begin?
As fish made their way, I tried to join in,
But a wave knocked me over, and I drowned in my spin!

Footprints in the Serene Sand

Tiny footprints lead to a prankster crab,
Who pinched my toe while I tried to nab,
A sun-tan that's golden, or so I hadthought,
Now it's red like a lobster, the lesson is taught!

With each step I took, the seagulls would warn,
Of flip-flops flying like the calm of a storm.
I chased them in circles, oh what a sight,
My footprints erased, oh what a delight!

The Horizon's Unwritten Poetry

The horizon beckons with a cheeky smile,
Promising wonders that might take a while.
With thoughts in the sand and giggles afloat,
I pondered my burger instead of my boat!

I wrote poetry in shells, words with a twist,
But the tide had other plans, like a sea's great assist.
My masterpiece washed away, oh that sly sea,
Guess I'll just stick to my burger and tea!

Calm Reflections of a Wandering Mind

Mirrors of water, where thoughts go astray,
I pondered my snack, like a jellyfish ray.
With a donut in hand, and a smile like a fool,
I sat on the shore, making splashes in the pool!

Inhale the salt air, exhale the deep sighs,
While fish compete for my half-eaten fries.
A moment of peace? Well, maybe my snack,
For I lost my zen, but found my food hack!

The Palette of Coastal Memories

A shore of laughter in the sun,
Where jellyfish dance and seagulls run.
The waves clap hands, a clumsy cheer,
Splashing like kids with no real fear.

Lost flip-flops tell tales in the sand,
While sideways crabs perform a band.
The breeze plays tricks with my wet hair,
I giggle as it sends me to despair.

Bikini edges tumble and slip,
As I take a silly, soggy dip.
With sunburned cheeks and ice cream stash,
I'm living dreams while posing for a splash.

Oh, the memory painted bright and bold,
Of beachside tales that never get old.
With laughter echoing into the blue,
The canvas of joy feels brand new.

Drifted Thoughts on Swaying Grass

The grass is tall, a soft green wave,
Where tumbleweeds seem quite misbehave.
Thoughts drift like clouds in a curious dance,
As squirrels lead a nutty romance.

Picnic ants march in a single line,
Crumbs of pizza seem divine.
Sun hats fly high with a gusty cheer,
Chasing after, my lunch disappears!

The breeze whispers secrets, soft and sweet,
While I frown at birds and their cheating feat.
They swoop and dive for my strawberry tart,
Oh, these feathered thieves, they steal my heart!

Drifting until the clock ticks slow,
With giggling friends that steal the show.
Bright days painted like a playful sketch,
Life's simple joys, forever they fetch.

Sailboats Adrift in Meditation

Sailboats bob like ducks all day,
Whispering secrets in their own way.
A captain yawns, with such little care,
As a seagull plots for snacks to share.

Wavy horizons play peek-a-boo,
While jellybeans float—oh, wouldn't you?
With soup cans clanking, making a dance,
The ocean's rhythm is pure happenstance.

Pirates dream of treasure on a whim,
But it's just a shell that's gleaming slim.
The anchor's stuck; it won't let me be,
As I laugh at my plight—what's wrong with me?

Finding zen in the bob of the tide,
With rudderless hopes and laughter as guide.
These ships adrift sail not for the fight,
But for giggles and sails that take flight.

Sandcastles of the Heart

In a kingdom built of grains and giggles,
Where seaweed wands and mermaid tickles.
I fortify my lofty hall,
With seashells, dreams, and kiddie squalls.

A bucket shatters, oh what a sight,
A sandstorm of giggles, pure delight.
My moat is a puddle, a leaky boat,
And I scream as my castle just starts to float!

Not every tower stands tall and proud,
With stray frisbees flying, oh, how they cloud!
Sand dollars dance as I stroke the moat,
A lost flip-flop tries to make a boat!

Yet in this mess, my heart finds cover,
With laughter and sand hugs, we're in love, oh brother!
So here's to castles with a sprinkle of cheer,
In the kingdom of hearts, there's nothing to fear.

The Stillness Between the Swells

Fish are doing yoga, in a finny pose,
Crabs are cracking jokes, in their little clothes.
Seagulls play charades, with feathers all afluff,
While waves just giggle, claiming they're not tough.

Turtles are slow dancing, under the soft sun,
Sandy toes are tapping, having way too much fun.
Shells are spinning tales, of their oceanic dreams,
And lobsters in sunglasses, plotting crazy schemes.

Horizon's Embrace at Dusk

The sun wears a mustache, on its way to bed,
Crabs throw a party, for the weary head.
Fish are swapping stories, of their daring escape,
While seaweed waltzes, in a flapper shape.

Starfish are photographers, capturing the scene,
As dolphins do cartwheels, looking quite obscene.
The tide's got a punchline, ready for a laugh,
While the moon snickers softly, in its silvery half.

Misty Mornings and Calm Waters

Morning fog is giggling, hiding all the sights,
While otters are mischief-makers, having water fights.
Seashells are gossiping, sharing salty tales,
And every wave whispers, like it knows all the fails.

Pelicans are pilots, flying upside down,
Trying to locate, the lost clownfish crown.
The sunrise is blushing, at this silly show,
With a wink and a chuckle, it begins to glow.

Clouds Softly Cradling the Coast

Fluffy clouds are napping, draped over the shore,
Each puff full of laughter, wanting to explore.
Waves are sneaky dancers, tapping to the beat,
While plankton hold a concert, beneath their tiny feet.

Wind whispers secrets, tickling the breeze,
Whales are serenading, with their deep, croaky keys.
Starfish paint their toenails, in colors quite bright,
As sunsets paint the ocean, in vibrant delight.

Lighthouses and the Poetry of Light

Standing tall with a silly grin,
They flash and twirl, doing a spin.
Guiding boats with a wink so sly,
Watching seagulls as they fly by.

They wear their stripes with utmost pride,
But their real talent? A lighthouse slide!
Tripping over rocks, they laugh and sway,
Lighting up the night, come what may.

The Quietude of Conch Shells

Whispering secrets from the deep,
Conch shells giggle as they sleep.
They hold the tales of the deep blue,
And often call beachgoers 'who knew?'

With a twist and a turn, they sing a song,
Their tunes are silly, where do they belong?
They roll in the waves, can't catch a break,
Just lounging around, it's a conch-shell fate.

Radiance of a Fading Day

Sunsets paint the sky in hues,
Flaming orange or bright blues.
As the day waves goodbye with flair,
The crabs applaud from their sandy chair.

Clouds sport shades of cotton candy,
While boats bob gently, a tad too dandy.
The laughter of kids echoes above,
As night creeps in with a shimmery glove.

Breathing Deep in Coastal Air

In the salty breeze, a whiff of fun,
The fish all giggle, 'We're number one!'
Seagulls squawking, not shy in the least,\nDemanding morsels, it's a feast!

Wave after wave, they splash and frolic,
In search of treasures, oh, how symbolic.
With sunscreen faces, they frolic and play,
Breathing in laughter, it's a beach day!

Silken Tides at Twilight

The waves roll in, a gentle tease,
Whispers of ocean, a salty breeze.
Seagulls squawk, they steal my fry,
I laugh and watch as they flit by.

With toes in sand, I wiggle and dance,
A crab scuttles past; oh, do take a chance!
Splashing about, I lose my flip-flop,
Chasing it down, I trip and I plop.

Sunset dip paints the sky with flair,
As jellyfish float without a care.
They wobbly jig, a gelatinous groove,
While I try to dance, they make me move!

The tide comes in, like a sneaky guest,
Waves chase my towel, I must confess.
I roll with laughter, soaked to the bone,
The ocean's prank has me in its throne.

The Song of the Endless Horizon

A boat named 'Lunch' sails forth with glee,
Packed with snacks, oh dear, let it be!
Pirates of old would shiver with fright,
When they smell the chips, so crunchy, so right.

The sun beats down, my hat takes flight,
It's off to dance with gulls in the light.
I run like a fool, arms flapping wide,
The wind just laughs as my hat starts to glide.

Horizons stretch with a curious face,
A whale flukes up; such a clumsy grace!
He winks at the gulls, and I hear them say,
"Check out that splasher, what a droll display!"

Sandcastles rise like dreams from the tide,
But the waves cackle, "Come, let's collide!"
I cheer them on as they claim their prize,
While moaning clams sing their funny goodbyes.

Melodies in the Mist

The fog rolls in like a snoozy cat,
Clouds blanket the beach, where's my sun hat?
A dolphin pops through with a splashy grin,
"Hey buddy, care to join in?"

With mist all around, I twist and shout,
Finding my friend who's nearly wiped out.
Her cooler's afloat, like a ship lost at sea,
While I giggle hard, it's just her and me.

Seashells sing songs, all polished and bright,
Every clam has a tale about seaweed fights.
They twist and twirl like a crazy ballet,
Each scoop of sand keeps the soggy at bay.

As laughter rises with the tides ebbing slow,
I toss a few shells to the waves below.
"Catch this one, you blubbery dude!"
With each splash, my heart sings in the neighborhood.

Unraveling Clouds above the Coast

The clouds above play a raucous game,
One looks like a dog, the other's a flame.
With goggles on, I squarely glare,
"Let's build a raft and ride the air!"

The wind jumps in, with a cheeky laugh,
Sweeping my snacks on its daring path.
Popcorn flies like confetti in June,
"Who wants to munch on a pesky balloon?"

Above, the seagulls take bets on my hat,
While I lunge forward, flat like a mat.
In the midst of the fun, I hear a loud roar,
"Hold on to your snacks, or they'll be no more!"

As the sun dips low, I strike quite a pose,
With sand in my hair, and a face full of nose.
The tides crash in, like laughter they chase,
While I wave goodbye to the clouds in their race.

Whispers of the Ocean Breeze

Seagulls giggle as they dive,
Crabs tap dance, alive and jive.
Waves complain like grumpy cats,
While sunbathers flop like silly mats.

Flip-flops flapping, on the run,
Sandy toes chase after fun.
Beach balls bounce with gleeful zest,
Even seaweed wears a fest!

Turtles laugh in a slow race,
Splashing water, what a pace!
Wet dogs shake, like they're on cue,
Life's a joke when waves are blue.

Pine trees sway with ocean's song,
Where all the wacky creatures throng.
Mermaids giggle 'neath the tide,
As fish compete with a joyful glide.

Tranquil Tides and Gentle Dreams

Chairs tipped over, drinks take flight,
Sunscreen battles in the bright light.
Children giggle, castles high,
As seagulls swoop down from the sky.

Sandy snacks turn into paste,
Mice in the sand make quite a haste.
Footprints zigzag, oh what a trail,
As clowns make waves, a comical sail.

Vibrant umbrellas flip around,
In the laughter, joy is found.
With every splash, the giggles fly,
Let's see who can make seagulls cry!

Bikinis wobble in the breeze,
And belly laughs come like a tease.
The tide rolls in with playful glee,
Here's to fun, oh let it be!

Embrace of the Horizon's Calm

Waves tickle toes, a playful tease,
Fish join in, inviting ease.
Sunburnt cheeks laugh in delight,
While waves crash down with silly might.

Umbrellas dance, take to the sky,
With ice cream dreams just passing by.
A beach ball rolls, but who will win?
It's all a game made of dolphin grin!

The lighthouse winks at seashells found,
While crabs complain, they just want ground.
Sandy sandwiches, a tasty treat,
All this joy makes life so sweet.

In flip-flops, we prance on the shore,
Riding the waves, we always want more.
As day turns dusk, stars take their place,
Nature's laughter in this funny space.

Starlight Reflections on Water

Moonlight twinkles on the crest,
Jellyfish wiggle, they love the jest.
Tides giggle as they play peek-a-boo,
And stargazers yell, 'I see you too!'

Beach bonfires crackle all night,
With marshmallows ready for a tasty bite.
As shadows dance, we feel the cheer,
What secrets do the stars hold dear?

Laughter mingles with ocean's hum,
Little fish tag, while big fish run.
Coconut hats fly, oh what a sight,
As we embrace the magical night.

Waves whisper tales of sailors bold,
Filling our hearts with stories untold.
Under the stars, we dance and sway,
Grateful for this funny, joyful play.

Tranquil Waters

The fish wear tiny hats, quite chic,
While dolphins dance and play hide and seek.
The seaweed laughs in a gentle sway,
As crabs parade in a fine, funky way.

A seagull struts, quite proud of his dish,
Claiming a sandwich, oh what a wish!
The tides giggle as they crash and retreat,
Whispering secrets in laughter so sweet.

Timeless Moments

A clam told a joke that fell quite flat,
While lazy otters lounged with a hat.
Snails in shades move at a slow pace,
Dreaming of races with grace and space.

The sun plays peekaboo, now a friend,
As sandcastles tumble, no need to mend.
Turtles gossip about who's the best,
In a game of card sharks, they're quite the jest.

The Serenity of Surging Waves

The waves wear wigs, all fluffy and bright,
Rolling in rhythm, a comical sight.
Starfish are giggling, some funny old fools,
As they break dance on glittery pools.

The tide pulls back with a playful scoff,
As a walrus drops in with a loud, cheeky cough.
Two jellyfish waltz in a shifting mist,
While crabs form a band that no one can resist!

Drift Away on a Breath of Wind

The kitefish fly high, their colors ablaze,
Chasing the seagulls in silly, wild ways.
The wind whispers jokes that elicit a laugh,
As boats bob along in a wobbly bath.

A beach ball giggles, bouncing around,
Making friends with the sand on the ground.
The afternoon sun wears a big, goofy grin,
As laughter echoes, letting good times begin.

Peaceful Chimes of Ocean's Lullaby

The shells tell tales of a pirate's dream,
Where sea cucumbers plot and scheme.
The starry night shines with shimmering glow,
As fish moonwalk under the moon's soft show.

The breeze plays the flute, a melodic tease,
While seahorses twirl in a whimsical freeze.
With sand in their toes, everyone rejoices,
In the hush of the night, laughter is our voice.

Horizon's Palette of Restful Colors

Painted skies with hues so bright,
A crab wears shades, a silly sight.
Wavelets tickle toes with glee,
While fish play tag beneath the sea.

Sunscreen's scent fills the warm breeze,
As laughter floats with utmost ease.
A seagull steals some chips and flies,
While beach balls bounce, oh what a prize!

Kites twist high in a playful race,
As sandcastles hold their sandy grace.
A shell sings tunes that make you grin,
Where the fun tales of the beach begin.

As waves roll in like a gentle sigh,
Palm trees dance, they reach for the sky.
A flip-flop flops and takes a leap,
While sunbathers dream in sun-soaked sleep.

A Dance of Dunes and Waves

Dunes waltz gracefully, what a show,
As beach balls bounce, and giggles flow.
Waves shimmy in a foamy spree,
And sand crabs host a jiggly jamboree.

Children scream as they chase a kite,
Hats take flight, what a comical sight!
A dog digs deep, all paws and cheer,
While surfboards dance like surfers near.

Footprints create a sketchy art,
As flip-flops fly, they play their part.
The sun sets low, a golden treasure,
As laughter echoes, pure pleasure.

Shells sparkle like jewels on the sand,
A clam waves back with a tiny hand.
Under the sky where fun meets the sea,
Life's a beach, oh how silly and free!

Quietude in the Foam's Embrace

Foamy whispers greet the shore,
As beach bums nap, but snore no more.
A jellyfish glides with grace and flair,
While starfish chuckle without a care.

Shells hold secrets in sandy beds,
While the ocean plays with our heads.
A crab holds court with a wave's salute,
Strutting sideways in a funny suit.

Mysterious tides, a playful tease,
Dancing shadows beneath the trees.
A sun hat sails, lost to the breeze,
While seaweed sways with elegant ease.

The horizon blushes, pink and blue,
As dolphins leap in a joyous crew.
Where fun meets tranquility, we sway,
A coastal bliss, hip-hip-hooray!

Seagulls' Songs on the Softest Air

Seagulls sing a cheeky tune,
As they dive down with a swoop and swoon.
Surfboards bob like boats in play,
While shells gossip about the day.

The tide rolls in, just like a grin,
As kids splash and let the fun begin.
The lifeguard yawns, just once more,
Watching swimmers explore the shore.

Footprints mingle, a jumbled art,
As the sun tosses hues, like it's smart.
Bubbles float on a gentle breeze,
With laughter echoing through the trees.

A parrot spies on the beachy scene,
Whispering jokes, oh so keen.
With every wave, joy takes the lead,
As fun takes root, exactly what we need!

Beneath the Celestial Canopy

Stars above like winking eyes,
Waves whisper jokes, beneath moonlit skies.
A crab in a tux, so dapper and spry,
Says, 'Life's a beach, come give it a try!'

Seagulls dive with flair and a cheer,
While dolphins dance, full of good cheer.
A clam tells tales of the tides with a grin,
As fish throw parties in their underwater kin.

The lighthouse blinks with a giggle or two,
'Who needs a map when you've got a view?'
Golden sands tickle toes in delight,
In this nighttime play, everything feels right.

Calm Shores at Dusk

The sun bows down with a painted grin,
Waves try to tickle, but they never win.
A sandcastle stands, but it leans to one side,
'I'm just a little drunk,' the sand says with pride.

Footprints in sand, a treasure trail,
While crabs practice tango, all to prevail.
Someone steps back, slips, then takes flight,
Lands right by seaweed – oh what a sight!

Kites soar high, full of glee,
While seagulls steal fries – oh what a spree!
Laughter and splashes, a silly parade,
At dusk on the shore, all worries do fade.

The Lullaby of Ocean Breezes

Whispers of wind tell secrets so sly,
Shells hold rendezvous, under a bright sky.
A fish with a hat, sipping juice through a straw,
Says, 'Life's just a splash, what could be the flaw?'

The tides tap-dance in rhythm and rhyme,
While seaweed waves at the pretty clear dime.
A pelican swoops, looking for fun,
'Who ordered this buffet? I'm not on the run!'

Children laugh, building heights that will fall,
Meanwhile, a sea turtle has seen it all.
'Life's like a beach ball, it bounces around,
You never know where joy will be found!'

Reflections on Still Waters

The lake shimmers bright, like a giant mirror,
A duck in a top hat says, 'Come hither!'
Turtles are sunbathing, plotting a prank,
While frogs jump in joy, their plans go to flank.

A fish with a mustache swims through a maze,
'Just don't feed me pizza, it makes me amaze!'
The reeds sway gently, to a dance unknown,
As dragonflies giggle, vibrating their tone.

Sunsets dye the sky in shades of delight,
Grumpy old fish complain, 'Why not at night?'
Ribbons of laughter ripple and twirl,
Nature's a show, come give it a whirl!

The Lure of Quiet Waters

The seagulls squawk, a comic show,
They steal my fries, oh what a blow!
The fish swim by, they wink and tease,
While I relax, enjoying the breeze.

A crab in a tux glides past my seat,
Is he on a date? Now that's a feat!
The sun's a jester, with rays that jest,
I laugh aloud, feeling quite blessed.

The waves bring bubbles, look here, they pop!
Like silly balloons, they don't ever stop.
I dare to join on this floaty quest,
With laughter and joy—oh, isn't life the best?

Here's to the ocean, a fun-filled spree,
Where worries dissolve in salty jubilee.
With every splash, a giggle takes flight,
And all my cares vanish into the night.

Ebbing Thoughts in Tidepools of Tranquility.

The tide pulls back with a playful grin,
And in the pools, the fun begins.
A starfish sits wearing a tiny hat,
While a crab performs a wiggly chat.

I ponder life as I dip my toes,
While a fish yawns widely, striking a pose.
The seaweed dances, a silly ballet,
Who knew the ocean could be this way?

With each ripple, my thoughts careen,
A turtle chuckles, oh what a scene!
I scoop up sand, it slips right through,
Like my fleeting ideas that won't renew.

But laughter lingers in the air, it's clear,
Every splash holds a tickle of cheer.
In joyous silence, I find my peace,
In these tidepools, worries cease.

Whispers of the Tide

The waves whisper secrets, oh can you hear?
A dolphin's joke makes the shoreline cheer.
On sandy carpets, I wiggle my toes,
While wave after wave offers up more shows.

A jellyfish floats with elegance and flair,
It wiggles and jiggles without a care.
With laughter erupting, the sun beams bright,
As I join the fun in this watery light.

A conch shell sings songs, oh isn't it grand?
While crabs play tag, oh, life is well-planned!
In this bubbly world, giggles collide,
With whispers of laughter each time they glide.

So here I stay, in joyous delight,
As ocean adventures stretch into night.
With each wave crashing, I smile with glee,
For in these soft whispers, I'm silly and free.

Echoes of Tranquil Waves

The wavelets giggle as they bounce and break,
A friendly splash, oh what a lake!
Seashells gather for a dance party loud,
As I dance along, feeling blissfully proud.

The sun beams down with a bright, cheeky wink,
As seagulls gossip, not missing a blink.
I join the chorus, with a silly tune,
Of mermaids' laughter beneath the moon.

A beach ball rolls, it's headed my way,
What's this? A dolphin's here to play!
With flip-flop footprints on warm golden sand,
I chase the tide—it's all so grand!

So let the waves echo this joyous spree,
Each splash a giggle, wild and carefree.
In this watery wonder, I'll always be,
Where fun fills the air, so blissfully.

The Serenity of Seafoam and Shells

Waves giggle as they kiss the shore,
Sandcastles pop like bubblegum galore.
A crab scuttles by with a sideways dance,
While seagulls eye fries, hoping for a chance.

Turtles race snails, who's winning the heat?
Seashells whisper secrets, oh so sweet.
A dolphin jumps high, with a cheeky flair,
Splashing a kid who's combing her hair.

The beach ball rolls off with a squeaky yelp,
While sunscreen becomes a slippery kelp.
Kids run like penguins, arms wide for flight,
As the sun sets low, painting the night.

And as laughter echoes, waves sing their tune,
A picnic of snacks beneath the full moon.
Pineapple hats worn with style and grace,
In this quirky haven, we find our place.

Gentle Currents of Hope

The tide pulls back a giant spoon,
Ready to serve waves as bright as a balloon.
Fish peek out, sporting sunglasses,
While starfish applaud from their sandy plazas.

A boat with a dragon sails by with pride,
While turtles judge the dolphins' joyride.
The wind tickles cheeks, making them grin,
As the sun plays tag on the horizon's skin.

Seagulls take selfies, phones in their beak,
While starfish show off their best winning streak.
The ocean's a stage, a wacky charade,
Where laughter and waves often serenade.

Lifesavers cheer, the beachgoers sway,
As jellyfish moonwalk, hip hip hooray!
When the sun dips low, a slumber party starts,
With sand between toes and warmth in our hearts.

Harbors of Stillness and Light

Boats bob like corks in a vast, blue stew,
While a whale splashes, yelling, "Look at this view!"
The lighthouse winks as it tops off a pie,
With flavors like berries that float through the sky.

A crab plays chess with a wise old fish,
"Checkmate!" he yells, fulfilling his wish.
Beach towels bloom like flowers in spring,
While a toddler sneezes, making seashells ring.

Seagulls hold a fashion show, strutting their stuff,
In tattered beachwear that's quite the tough cuff.
As night shades the world in a blanket of stars,
Frogs moonlight serenade from nearby guitars.

In this harbor of laughter, joy doesn't cease,
Where waves sing enchantment, and we find our peace.
A magician flips fish from the sea to our hands,
In a landscape so whimsical, where dreams make their plans.

Beneath the Canopy of Clouds

Under soft shadows, the ocean's our stage,
Clouds giggle lightly, releasing their rage.
Sunscreen warriors set forth to defend,
Against sneaky sand that seems to transcend.

A lobster sunbathes in shades of mauve,
While clam shells gossip, in heaps they dissolve.
Kites soar above, drawing laughter and cheer,
As kids eat ice cream, with sticky delight near.

Beach chairs recline, like old pals at rest,
While a dog starts "fetching" the wrong kid's vest.
The sun's a big flirt, peeking through the mist,
Making shadows dance in a whimsical twist.

As the day rolls on, a party begins,
With sand between fingers and freedom in spins.
The world fades away, wrapped in laughter's embrace,
Beneath the soft clouds, we find our own space.

Awakened by the Roll of the Surf

Morning sun spills like jam on toast,
Waves whisper secrets like an ocean's ghost.
Seagulls squawk jokes, so loud and spry,
While beach chairs dance as the tide rolls by.

The sand tickles toes, a stubborn pest,
Trying to steal naps, oh what a jest!
Flip-flops chase crabs in a game of tag,
As sunscreen fails and the beach bags sag.

Children giggle, with buckets in tow,
Building sandcastles, putting on a show.
But the tide waves hello, crashes the walls,
"Your kingdom's doomed!" it comically calls.

Laughter echoes as we splash and run,
Flip-flops flying, oh what's the fun?
With salt on our lips and mischief in air,
The day's simple pleasures, nothing can compare.

Stillness in Every Tide

The ocean glimmers like grandma's best dress,
Waves have a rhythm, I must confess.
They dance a soft jig, a sea shanty tune,
While beach balls float like inflatable moons.

A crab in a snapper wears mom's old shoe,
Pretending he's stylish, oh what a view!
Sunbathers lie still, as if under a spell,
While the sun thinks it's funny, can't you tell?

Seagulls plotting from high above skies,
Chasing their dreams, or fries with surprise.
Each gust of breeze brings laughter, it seems,
Nature's a joker, with whimsical schemes.

So we gather our towels, bringing cheer,
As sand drifts like snowflakes, quite sincere.
With every wave's whisper, a grin spreads wide,
A perfect calm, where joy can't hide.

Seafoam Dreams and Coastal Calm

Seafoam giggles as it tickles our feet,
A bubbly companion, oh what a treat!
Fishes flip-flap like they're in a race,
With rubber duckies, they're never misplaced.

On sandy shores, we build our delight,
A castle of shells that's quite a sight.
But the tide's a sneaky friend in disguise,
Wave crashes come with a splash in the eyes.

Beneath a bright sun, we stretch out and yawn,
While jellyfish blanket the front lawn.
They float by us wearing hats, how absurd,
As if they're the life of the beach, how absurd!

Laughter cascades with the day's final light,
We gather the sea's treasures, all feels alright.
With pockets of sand and hearts full of glee,
What a ludicrous day spent right by the sea!

Gentle Embrace of Evening Light

As twilight tiptoes, the waves dim their song,
Stars peek through clouds, joining the throng.
The breeze brings whispers, soft and low,
Jellybeans tumble like waves, oh what a show!

The moon's a big smile, shining so bright,
While fish pull a prank in the shimmering night.
They splash and they dart, in a sea of delight,
Turning dinner plans into a comical fright.

Shells gather round, gossiping away,
About the day's antics, come join in the play!
Sandcastles topple, laughter's the goal,
As beachgoers sing, playful and whole.

With marshmallow dreams in the curling dusk,
The ocean keeps chuckling, so wild and brusque.
In the glow of night, we all share the same,
As the coast whispers softly, laced with a name.

Moonlight Caressing Coral Sands

The moon sneezed in the night, oh what a sight,
Fighting off waves with a watery bite.
Crabs dance on the shore, with a tap-tap game,
While the seaweed giggles, calling them names.

A jellyfish floats with a jiggle and jive,
As the starfish watches, feeling quite alive.
Where the tide takes a break, and shells start to sing,
The lobsters join in, doing their bling-bling.

A lighthouse blinks like a disco ball,
As seagulls swoop down, their hair in a sprawl.
The waves clap their hands, a humorous show,
As fish flip and flop, putting on a glow.

So let's raise our cups made of sand and foam,
For this goofy beach life is our seagull home!

Gentle Respite by the Shore

The sun's on a break, taking naps on the waves,
While crabs have a meeting, plotting their braves.
Seashells whisper jokes, a conch with a grin,
As dolphins do flips in their watery kin.

A sea cucumber winks, "I'm cooler than you!"
As starry-eyed fish say, "We're artists too!"
The sand feels like plush, oh yes, what a thrill,
As the tide rolls in, with a tickle and frill.

Seagulls gather 'round, sharing tales like a club,
While a hermit crab struts, "I'm rocking this grub!"
Tidal pools laugh, with a splash and a dash,
Creating a scene that's more funny than sash!

So let's toast with cocktails, the ocean our mate,
In this carnival of waves, life's taking the bait!

Where the Sky Kisses the Sea

Clouds play tag with the gulls in the air,
While fish in the waves all rejoice without care.
The sunset's a painter with colors so bold,
While sea lions joke, "We're young, bright, and old!"

A pelican swoops down, it's a comical flight,
With fish in its beak, it's a dinner delight.
The hermit crabs spin like they're in a race,
While the sea breeze giggles, blowing right in their face.

Waves hum a tune, with a splash and a cheer,
As the sun whispers secrets, for all to hear.
The seaweed joins in, with a swish and a sway,
In this oceanic ballet, they dance and they play.

So let's laugh at the sea, with its rollicking fun,
Under skies that blush as the day's coming done!

Driftwood Dreams

The driftwood's a champion, the king of the sand,
With barnacles posing, making a band.
Seashells are dancers in a glittering show,
While sunbeams are spotlights that shimmer and glow.

Anglerfish throw parties, all the creatures arrive,
With octopuses twisting, so lively, they thrive.
In puddles of laughter, the crabs juggle clams,
As the tide rolls in, they dodge all the jams.

A prancing seahorse wearing a hat, so chic,
Sways to the rhythm, all fancy and sleek.
The waves laugh along, with a tickle and tease,
As fish pull pranks, saying, "Can we all please?"

So here's to the beach, with its giggles and schemes,
In this world of driftwood, we linger in dreams!

Beneath the Whispering Palms

The palms dance like they're in a play,
While crabs clap shells without delay.
Seagulls squawk in chorus so loud,
I can't help but laugh, oh how proud!

A turtle strolls, oh what a sight,
Takes a selfie, "I'm just right!"
With coconuts in a game of toss,
I think they've missed, oh what a loss!

Kids build castles, with moats so deep,
While dodging waves that come like a leap.
Their sandman is sculpted with flair,
But alas! He lost his hair!

Waves whisper jokes to the sandy shore,
While crabs tap dance, always wanting more.
Nature's comedy, a whimsical spree,
Underneath the palms, so carefree!

Nature's Tranquil Canvas

The sky wears hues of cotton candy dreams,
While dolphins play and burst with gleams.
The sun dips low, donning shades of gold,
   As gulls share secrets, a story retold.

Here, the sea laughs, it bubbles with joy,
   Playing tricks on a sunbathing boy.
With splashy waves and wiggly fish,
   They plot mischief—what a dish!

A beach ball bounces off a sand mound,
And slices through laughter, oh such sound!
While crabs in tuxedos dance in a line,
   They twirl and spin, it's truly divine!

And as the moon rises, so bright and wide,
   Starfish gather, wearing their pride.
A wink from the tide, a chuckle and cheer,
   Nature's canvas, where joy is clear!

Pathways of the Ocean Wind

The breeze is cheeky, it tickles my nose,
As sand flies past like invisible prose.
With flip-flops squeaking upon the path,
I'm joined by a dog, prone to bath!

The ocean calls, "Come join the fun!"
As waves rise high, watching the sun.
I tripped on a shell, did a funny dance,
While fish nearby gave me a glance!

Wind plays tricks with my floppy hat,
As seabirds caw, "We don't want that!"
They circle around and tease my hair,
I can't help but giggle, floating without care!

With laughter swirling, like a gusty breeze,
The joy is boundless, as I catch my tease.
On these pathways where the sea does wend,
The wind tells tales of joy to send!

Distant Horizons of the Mind

Look afar, where the sky meets the swell,
A horizon whispers, "Can you tell?"
The waves giggle, a ripple of cheer,
A vacation spot that feels so near.

I spot a fisherman, asleep with a pole,
Dreaming of treasures, oh what a goal!
The fish hold a meeting, plotting their escape,
"Let's swim like ninjas, make him gape!"

Sandy toes wiggling, I dash to the edge,
As the tide giggles, a playful hedge.
A mermaid holds court, "Who's next for a splash?"
She laughs, saying, "Come on, let's clash!"

As night falls softly, the stars give a wink,
Trying to nudge me, wise as I think.
Distant horizons that tickle my mind,
Paint pictures of laughter, so gently aligned!

Secrets in the Salt-Kissed Air

The seagulls squawk, oh what a choir,
As beach balls bounce with endless desire.
A crab in shades, struts like a star,
While sunscreen's scent floats near and far.

Flip-flops flapping on sandy toes,
Laughter spills like ocean flows.
A toddler's tantrum, ice cream drop,
Oh, the joy of a sandy mop!

Kites dance high, with tangled string,
As jellyfish take their lazy fling.
Fish whispers joke beneath the tide,
Where sandcastles keep secrets untried.

In salty breezes, chuckles thrive,
While algae blooms make surfers dive.
With every splash, the giggles grow,
As beach-side tales begin to flow.

Lullabies of the Rolling Waves

The tide rolls in with a soft embrace,
Paddling dogs have a splishy splash race.
A floatie donut spins like a wheel,
While kids invent games we can't conceal.

Waves whisper secrets of salty delight,
As sunburned noses begin to ignite.
The crabs in tuxedos, a fancy parade,
While sunscreen battles its sticky crusade!

Shells like treasures in nooks they hide,
As flip-flop footprints walk side by side.
With each soft thud, the waters laugh,
Rolling tides serve an oceanic graph.

The noon sun nods, it's time for a snack,
With chips and dips we barely unpack.
As bellyaches from laughter combine,
Each wave adds fun, like a glinting sign.

Silken Sands Beneath the Moonlight

Moonlight dances on shimmering tides,
As the night reveals what silliness hides.
A cat on a raft, what a curious sight,
Chasing her tail in the pale moonlight.

The beach bonfire flickers and glows,
While marshmallows roast and giggly prose.
A ghost crab struts in a moonlit suit,
Pretending to be some fancy brute!

With laughter echoing along the shore,
And tales of the day that leave us wanting more.
A sand angel yawns, ready for dreams,
As ocean waves weave whimsical themes.

While shadows flicker, a shadowed prank,
A snoozing sunbather tipped off the plank.
The salty breeze hums a tune so clear,
Capturing giggles in the night air here!

A Symphony of Shells and Silence

Beneath the stars, a shell plays a tune,
Held by a child who sways like a loon.
Whales in pajamas float by so grand,
While starfish toss parties on golden sand.

Crabs on stage, in sand they perform,
Choreographed moves, oh what a norm!
Each wave claps softly, a rhythm so sweet,
To the dance of the shells, the night's heartbeat.

In the silent ocean, a ticklish breeze,
Whispers of laughter, like rustling leaves.
A crab with a hat, truly unique,
As tides groove together, cheek to cheek.

With shells as instruments, the night plays rare,
Jellyfish sway with an elegant flair.
While the sand tickles toes that roam,
In a world of shells, we feel right at home.

www.ingramcontent.com/pod-product-compliance
Lightning Source LLC
Chambersburg PA
CBHW072129070526
44585CB00016B/1596